Abundant Living

Two Truths Hidden in the Parable of the Sower Can Release You Into Abundant Life

Kevin Shorter

Acknowledgements

This book would not have been possible without my wife, Allison. It was her heart's passion to help orphan girls in China, and I got carried along for the incredible ride. Allison's love and support has given space for us to listen to God's leading for us and our family.

I'm also grateful for my two daughters, Rachel and Elizabeth, who helps us on our journey by asking for God's help along the way. Your willingness to adjust to our frequent changes and love of China – the people, language, and food – has helped us maintain our joy and passion.

Finally, I want to thank our financial supporters, board members, interns, and prayer partners of Josiah's Covenant who have made it possible to experience one of the greatest adventures we have had living this abundant life.

Table of Contents

Chapter 1

Why This Book?

In John 10:10 Jesus tells us He came that we may have life and life to the full, and during His time on earth, He demonstrated to us how to live this abundant life through His words and deeds. He is the way, the truth, and the life[1]. And yet, He could do nothing on His own, but only what He saw His Father doing[2].

What does this mean for us? If we want to live this abundant life that Jesus is offering, then we need to follow His example. Luke 8 spells this out for us by giving us two specific action points.

At the time that God was teaching me this concept, my family lived in China following a dream to create a family for teenage orphan girls. We followed this vision to a country we had never visited, not knowing the language, and having no connections. In under five years, we had accomplished more than we could have ever expected. We created a business entity to hire teenage orphan girls, were given a farm, renovated a three story, 24-room dorm and

---

[1] John 14:6
[2] John 5:19

kitchen unit, and successfully transitioned out by handing it over to local Chinese people to continue the ministry. Many of these things happened because we were attempting to follow these two principles which I intend to describe in the following pages.

God wants to use all of us in amazing ways. While the journey God has for you will look differently, His closeness and adventure for you will be no less exciting. I hope that this book will ignite passion in you to go after all that God has made available and be willing to accept nothing less than abundant living.

Chapter 2

The Parable of the Sower Revisited

Jesus Loved to Tell Stories

Jesus was a master storyteller. His insistence of using parables instead of just straightforward teaching has given preachers fodder for their sermons for two millennia. Oftentimes you can hear the same parable preached with differing action points pulled out, and each sermon might very well be what Jesus had in mind. Parables allow for this because they often leave the moral open for discussion. We can keep going back to a particular passage and find God touching our hearts in new and different ways.

And yet, there are some parables that get the same action points preached so often that we could miss what else Jesus may be trying to communicate. I believe this has happened with the parable of the sower.

Most often this parable is taught that the seed is the gospel and there are four ways people respond to it. It's basically taught as a salvation message and is great as such. People are encouraged to get their hearts right before God, so the gospel may take root in their lives.

However, for those of us who already believe, our only application seems to be to continue to sow seeds of the gospel that others may respond. While I don't want to negate this approach, allow for me to pull out a couple other interpretations that I believe will encourage you and lead you into the promised abundant life.

I want to particularly look at the version included in Luke 8:1-15. In this parable there was a farmer sowing seeds. It appears that he just throws his seed indiscriminately as it landed among four different types of soils. We should note that there is power in the seed no matter where it lands, because on every soil it landed, it tried to grow. While this is true, life is more readily released when it landed on good soil.

Let's look at how it reads in the NIV:

The Parable of the Sower – Luke 8: 1-15

After this, Jesus traveled about from one town and village to another, proclaiming the good news of the kingdom of God. The Twelve were with him, and also some women who had been cured of evil spirits and diseases: Mary (called Magdalene) from whom seven demons had come out; Joanna the wife of Chuza, the manager of Herod's household; Susanna; and many others. These women were helping to support them out of their own means.

While a large crowd was gathering and people were coming to Jesus from town after town, he told this parable: "A farmer went out to sow his seed. As he was scattering the seed, some fell along the path; it was trampled on, and the birds ate it up. Some fell on rocky ground, and when it came up, the plants withered because they had no moisture. Other seed fell among thorns, which grew up with it and choked the plants. Still other seed fell on good soil. It came up and yielded a crop, a hundred times more than was sown."

When he said this, he called out, "Whoever has ears to hear, let them hear."

His disciples asked him what this parable meant. He said, "The knowledge of the secrets of the kingdom of God has been given to you, but to others I speak in parables, so that,

"'though seeing, they may not see;

though hearing, they may not understand.'"

"This is the meaning of the parable: The seed is the word of God. Those along the path are the ones who hear, and then the devil comes and takes away the word from their hearts, so that they may not believe and be saved. Those on the rocky ground are the ones who receive the word with joy when they hear it, but they have no root. They believe for a while, but in the time of testing they fall away. The seed that fell among thorns stands for those who hear, but as they go on their way they are choked by life's worries, riches and pleasures, and they do not mature. But the seed on good soil stands for those with a noble and good heart, who hear the word, retain it, and by persevering produce a crop."

Chapter 3

The Word of God is Living and Active

What is the Seed Being Sown?

While we often take the seed as meaning the Gospel, the Bible states it is the message of the kingdom[3] and the word of God[4]. The message of the kingdom and the word of God are much broader than just the salvation message. Many of Jesus' parables start, "the kingdom of heaven is like..." and then goes onto explain it. The seed being spread are truths and principles of His kingdom. He wants us to know the message of the kingdom so that His kingdom will take root in our lives.

Our enemy also understands the principles of this parable. We catch a little of this in the explanation of how he snatches up the seed that lands on the hard soil. He knows there is power in the seed, so he does all he can to stop it. He first tries to remove seed. If it takes root, he then will try to stifle the growth of God's seed by sending his own seed or his weeds: trouble, persecution, worry, or lies.

---

[3] Matthew 13:19
[4] Luke 8:11

Our enemy uses this same principle of the sower to feed his own seed into our lives. He knows if he can get his seed into our soil, then we will start to manifest his kingdom instead of God's. He is not content with just removing God's seeds, but he is also adding his own into our fields.

The Seed in This Parable Are Thoughts or Ideas

The enemy is constantly feeding us lies in hopes that some of his seed will find soil to grow. Like the farmer in the parable, the enemy does not throw seed sparingly. This is why we are to take all of our thoughts captive and think on whatever is excellent and praiseworthy[5]. These thoughts become our behaviors[6]. They determine how much of the kingdom we are capable of manifesting.

It is the truth that sets us free; therefore, we need more good seed to release us from the effects of the bad seed. Lies are replaced by truth[7]. Evil is overcome by good[8]. Fear is driven out by love[9].

---

[5] 2 Corinthians 10:5 & Philippians 4:8
[6] James 1:15
[7] John 8:32

Let's sow the message of God's kingdom and speak the love of God into every circumstance. In every conversation, may we speak only what is helpful for building others up according to their needs, that it may benefit those who listen[10]. This is how we sow good seed.

What is the Word of God?

Going back to Luke 8, the passage clearly states in verse 11 that the seed in the parable is the word of God. But, what is the word of God?

When we look at Hebrews 4:12, we see that "the word of God is living and active, sharper than any two-edged sword." Often we are taught the Bible is the word of God. So, does this mean we are to spread the Bible everywhere on different soils? The Bible, or Scripture is the very breath of God showing us the heart and ways of God[11].

As before, I believe we limit the message in this Hebrews verse by only thinking of the Bible. The first four chapters of Hebrews

---

[8] Romans 12:21
[9] 1 John 4:18
[10] Ephesians 4:29
[11] 2 Timothy 3:16

describe how God spoke in the past, how the Israelites heard His voice, and how we are to pay attention to what we have heard.

Three times leading to the verse in chapter 4 verse 12, the author quotes Psalm 95:7-8: "Today, if you hear his voice, do not harden your hearts." The connotation of this passage is that the word of God is the voice of the Spirit communicating to you. It most definitely means the Scripture, but it also means so much more.

God is Always Sowing Seed

In the parable we are told that the sower scatters the seed indiscriminately. It goes out everywhere and often. The seed is the voice of God and it is always communicating[12]. We are created to hear His voice.

In the garden God strolled with Adam and continued to speak to him even after he sinned. It was Adam who hid himself, not God. Isaiah tells us he heard the voice of God "saying"[13] – ongoing words being spoken. God was already talking, Isaiah just had to tune himself to that

---

[12] Hebrews 1:1-2
[13] Isaiah 6:8

voice. In the Gospels, Jesus said that we are to recognize His voice[14].

Just as our enemy is constantly feeding us his seed as negative thoughts, God is constantly giving us His seed of His voice. This is why it is important to cultivate an ear for the voice of God and distinguish between these two sources of seed in our lives. One will lead us to life; the other will lead us to death[15]. It is our thoughts that will determine how much of God's kingdom will have in our lives.

I have found that listening to what the Spirit has to say illuminates what's in my heart that is keeping me from fully believing the truths of God. The Spirit, who searches our hearts, can reword the truths of God in ways that speak right into and past the pain and hurt in our lives for us to receive His truth.

How Does This Work?

In this world bad things happen. My cousin lost her three-month-old son to SIDs (sudden infant death syndrome). She went to wake him from sleep, and he was already gone. My brother suddenly died a few years ago leaving

---

[14] John 10:3,5
[15] John 10:10

behind his wife and three young kids. In the morning he went hiking with his daughter, and in the evening he had a seizure and never recovered. My good friend had his wife divorce him limiting access to his three sons to just weekends. People lose jobs; friends relocate and seemingly forget you; people slander you, steal from you, and at times deeply hurt you.

In the midst of pain, it is difficult to read Bible passages and believe God loves us, He has a plan for our lives, or that He wants to bless us. All we can feel and see is our pain.

Your pain may not be as drastic as losing a child or father or spouse. Your pain may be a food allergy that drastically limits what you can eat. You may have overwhelming debt and can't see your way out of it. It may be something that happened to you when you were young, and you think God didn't take care of you then, so you don't think you can trust Him now.

Whatever your pain, you are left with two options: 1. to separate parts of your heart from God fearing more pain or 2. to have an encounter with God that speaks into your pain and changes you, leading you to life, health, and peace. Choosing the first option deadens Christianity. Choosing the second option lives out Hebrews 4:12.

God Wants to Meet Us in Our Time of Need

God's word in this context is God speaking to reword His truth in ways that penetrate them past our pain and experiences so we can hear and believe Him. In His love for us, God enters into our pain in order that our relationship may be renewed.

I don't know the exact word each of you need to hear from God today, and I am not saying this is an easy step. What I am saying is that the voice of our Father is kind and gentle. He does not break the bent reed[16]. He goes after the lost sheep[17]. He never leaves nor forsakes us[18]. All of this is true because He loves us beyond what we can ever imagine possible. And, in His love He will come to us and meet us in our time of need. As we draw near to Him, He will draw near to us[19].

---

[16] Isaiah 42:3
[17] Luke 15:3-7
[18] Hebrews 13:5
[19] James 4:8

Chapter 4

What Every New Christian Needs to Know

What Every Child Needs?

It's so important we hear the voice of God. When children enter the world, the first thing they need is the love and attention from their parents. This attention to their needs, loving touches and emotional bonding build security into the child. This security provides safety for children to grow properly.

There was a story on America's National Public Radio a few years ago about a man who was born into a Romanian orphanage. In the 80's and 90's, these orphanages provided very little care for the orphans, many of whom were left alone in cribs for days on end without human connection. When the world started finding out about the situation, there were 100,000 children in these institutions, and it became clear that they had a wide range of mental and emotional problems. Here is a quote from the story: "Without someone who is a reliable source of attention, affection and stimulation the wiring of the brain goes awry.

The result can be long-term mental and emotional problems."[20]

What Does Every New Christian Need?

What became clear for me in this article is how new Christians are the same way. The first thing they need to know is how to connect with their Heavenly Father. They need to know how to hear His voice and to see how attentive He is on them, so that their brains would be wired to receiving His good intentions for them. Every Christians needs to know they are special to the Heavenly Father. I believe this is something we should teach every new Christian, how to hear the voice of their Heavenly Father for themselves.

In most follow-up material, we lead new Christians through the disciplines of the faith - assurance of salvation, how to study the Bible, the importance of fellowship, etc. While I like most of the material, it is like sending a kid to school without giving them a home first. All the teaching in the world will not overcome the

---

[20] https://www.npr.org/sections/health-shots/2014/02/20/280237833/orphans-lonely-beginnings-reveal-how-parents-shape-a-childs-brain/. Accessed July 31, 2015.

huge deficit created in the new believer that can't hear the voice of God on their own.

We Need to Recognize the Voice of God

Jesus said my sheep know My voice[21]. It is not limited to a select few. In fact, the sheep are supposed to run away from another's voice[22]. He is saying that each of us needs to know His voice to such a degree that we would recognize when we hear a different voice and move away from it. We need to spend time listening to Him. What does He sound like? What kind of words does He say?

Often we strongly encourage reading Scriptures because they are the very words of God. However, we don't equally encourage hearing God's voice. I believe the reason we don't do this is because we are afraid the enemy would easily lead these new believers astray. However, the truth is that the enemy is already speaking to these new believers, and they are already listening to him. They need to hear the voice of their Father to override those lies. The Father's words bring life not condemnation; they bring hope, not despair.

---

[21] John 10:3
[22] John 10:5

What This Has Looked Like for Me

When I was in China, I started a group specifically for the ex-pat men living in town. The group attracted men who lived in China for 10, 15, 20 years, and yet, I had only been there under one year when I started the group. These men were from England, Australia, New Zealand, Philippines, Finland, Canada, and the like. Thirty plus men from over ten countries were a part of this group at different times. These men had done wonderful things for the Lord in China and had respect outside our city.

While I felt God's leading to do this, I had to fight my insecurities. One guy in the group trained life coaches all over Asia, North America, and Europe. When we first started meeting, I felt like he would stare at me trying to figure out if I should be trusted. Another guy told me he didn't like half of what I was doing in group and didn't see the need for it. And another guy shared in group that I was just like every American who always felt they should be in charge.

I would leave group at times questioning myself and doubting if I really should be doing this. Each time, this would lead me to pray, and I kept feeling God's reassurance for me to start this group.

I would also call a good friend back in the US to verbalize my doubts knowing he believed in me and would encourage me. There was also a guy in the group I chose to trust early on, and I would confess my fears to him, as well.

My calls to these friends were not my need to be consoled; I didn't want those negative views to have a place to stick. I was fighting them by choosing not to ignore them but to bring them into the light. Each time I shared with these two friends, the sting of the insecurities became less, and I would strengthen my belief in God's call to lead this group.

As I continued the group, the men that came each week became close friends. One older gentleman said the group was the most significant thing he had experienced. It opened him up to other things God had for him. One mentioned how he was always giving to others, and this group gave him men who would give to him. Another man said his wife would keep encouraging him to come because she said he was a better husband when he went.

This group was one of the highlights of my time in China. And yet, I was tempted to give up on it early on. I fought those negative thoughts by listening again to God's word to me, confessing the lies I was hearing, hanging on by faith, and allowing God to use others to also speak His word to me.

In order to maintain good soil for the word of God to grow, we need to fight the weeds the enemy is sowing. We also need to water the word by continuing to come back to it and committing to believe in that word. If we don't allow people to learn how to hear the voice of God, they will never overcome the voice of the enemy.

Let us start to trust our Heavenly Father with raising His own children. Jesus wants us to come to Him. Without this attention and His words of life, we are like the orphaned children in the NPR story. Our brains will not be wired effectively for God's kingdom.

Chapter 5

How Does the Seed Take Root

The Seed is the Word of God

Back to Luke 8, the seed is the word of God. This phrase includes the gospel being preached, but it also includes the Bible. And, it includes anytime God wants to communicate to us. This communication is how I want to read this passage today.

With this in mind, there are four ways we can respond to God speaking to us. God may send us inspiration in our times of prayer or just in the midst of our day, and we doubt it is from God. This word hits hard ground, and the enemy steals the word from us. Other times we hear from God, and while we initially are encouraged, we don't follow through with the word and lose it. Still other times the word is pressed out of us because life tells us another story. Finally, we have the good soil that allows God's word to transform our lives.

The surprising truth is that we can maintain each of these four soils in our lives. For one word we hear from God, we may respond perfectly with good soil. But at another time we may hear something not as easy to accept and we are the rocky soil.

Abraham Changed Soils to Create Ishmael

Think of Abraham. He gets the word of the Lord that he will be a father of many nations and will have a son. And so, he holds onto this word for many years. It sits in good soil waiting for the fulfillment. He leaves all that he knows to follow this promise.

But then time passes, the pressures of the world and his old age start to choke out the word. He decides with his wife Sarah to use human logic instead of trusting the Lord. They reasoned that there are other ways for him to have a child other than only through Sarah. Therefore, he took Hagar and had a son, Ishmael. God had to come and remind Abraham that the promised son would come through Sarah. The "Ishmaels" we produce will have no place in the inheritance God promises to the seed that is produced in the good soil[23].

In the beginning we are often quick to listen to the word of the Lord. We are not sure what the will of God is for our lives, so we

[23] Galatians 4:30

constantly listen. However, after some time has passed, we think we should use our minds to put the plans together. This will generally lead us away to trust ourselves – not God's voice. We need to maintain good soil.

Elijah Changed Soils to Runaway

Think of Elijah. In the beginning, you see how he was full of good soil. He risks his life going before the king and queen to warn of a pending drought because of their rebellion. He trusts the Lord for provisions as the drought causes a famine in the land. He believes God will raise a boy back to life. Not to mention the whole show at Mount Carmel. He has prepared good soil and readily applies the word of God that He receives.

Then the enemy sent fear into Elijah's heart. After all these wonderful acts, Jezebel, the queen, promises to kill Elijah and fear enters his heart leading him to run away. Fear closed the door to hearing God's word, and any seed sent from the Father was stolen by the enemy. Thankfully, God leads Elijah to an encounter to bring him out of it.

New circumstances create new opportunities to hear from God. We must continually maintain our soil to stay fresh with Him and to live the abundant life.

Our Story of Different Soils

In the fall of 2012, my family was sidetracked by a word of the Lord to pick up our things and move to China. We didn't know what city or for what reason, but we were sure He said move. We started making plans and continued to listen intently for more answers. We finally felt led to a certain city to provide a family for teenage orphan girls. I feel His word landed on good soil – in four short months we left all we knew in America to believe Him for the unknown.

Fast forward a couple of years. We had been studying the language and building a base to do the things we felt led to do. In the midst of it all, we saw our personal finances going to zero with no real indication that that would change. Allison and I have been trained in some of the top practices on how to raise support, however, we felt very clearly that we were not to directly ask anyone to give to us. We could make it available, but we were not to use those tactics on which we had been trained.

I don't feel there is anything wrong with raising support, but God clearly wanted us to trust Him for our finances. I mention all of this because Allison and I had to continually go back to Him to confirm this direction. The temptation was to turn from the word to make it happen on our own. We wanted to gain more control and to gain the feeling of safety by striving to create a base of financial donors. We were tempted to create an Ishmael when God wanted to give us an Isaac.

The world may tell us we will run out of money, we will not have enough for our kids' education, or we will not be taken care of. The cares of providing financially for our family at times threatened to strangle the word. Like many of you, we are still on the journey, but the journey requires us to actively maintain good soil and listen for the word of God.

How God Provided for Us

At one point of the journey, my wife went back to the US to attempt to recruit interns. The girls and I stayed back in China to save on finances. When she returned to China, it was time to renew our visa to stay in the country. However, as we attempted to renew our visa, we were told we needed to get a different kind of visa because we were in process of creating a Chinese business.

This new visa option required our whole family to leave the country while requesting them. We scrambled to find flights and a hotel last minute during a major Chinese holiday travel time, so everything was at a premium. My wife and I were incredibly discouraged thinking how we were going to pay for it all.

When we prayed, we thought God was encouraging us to treat this unexpected trip as a vacation and enjoy this forced week-long visit to a neighboring Asian country. We chose to believe this was from God and did what you do on vacation - ate out, paid for tourist activities, and tried to enjoy ourselves.

When we got back to China after getting our new visa, doubt crashed in. Why didn't we just go on the cheap? While we did our best to celebrate God and thank Him for the nice vacation, we could see our bank statements didn't look good. We acknowledged the fear but tried to put our faith in what we felt God had led us to do.

The next day we got an email from a friend and supporter saying they received a bonus from work that they wanted to give to us. They didn't know about our unexpected trip or the feelings of uncertainty we had about our finances. But God did. And He not only provided for our vacation... He gave us double the money back.

I would like to say that the rest of the time in China we didn't struggle with money concerns. This was not the case. We were in negative cash flow for most of the time there. We flew through our savings and had several times where we were not sure if we would have enough. Then there were times like above where God let us know He hadn't forgotten us.

Another example of this was when we needed a van to go back and forth to our farm. We were barely making it each month, and the thought buying a vehicle was crazy to us. However, during this time we received a message from someone we didn't know offering to buy us a van.

It turned out that this lady received prayer from my wife when she was visiting a church. This couple decided to join our newsletter list and quietly had been following our journey. After a couple of years of watching us, they decided to give us the finances for the van.

Over the next couple years, they gave us over $50,000 which paid for the van, setting up a Chinese business, and renovating living quarters for the orphan girls. While we struggled over wanting to raise the finances for the ministry, God was quietly preparing the solution. His solution was more than a financial partner, they became a ministry partner helping us in many other ways. When we could only think of just enough, He had planned more than enough. When we wanted to produce an Ishmael, God was forming an Isaac.

The Good Soil Challenge

Think about the word God has given you. How is your soil? Have you turned from His voice because it seems too impossible? Have you tried to make it happen on your own? How many of us create Ishmaels because after hearing the word from the Lord, we try to think through how we will make it happen. The child of the slave woman is birthed by rationalizing God's plans. We move off the fertile soil to build instead of grow. These Ishmaels we create may have some success, but they will never share in the inheritance promised to the Isaacs God wants to give us[24].

---

[24] Galatians 4:30

The child of the free woman is birthed out of love and holding onto the promises of God - maintaining the good soil and allowing God to lead by His word. Therefore let us get rid of the slave woman and her son, for the slave woman's son will never share in the inheritance with the free woman's son[25]. Our inheritance is too big to ever try to comprehend it by logic and reason. God is able to do so much more than we can comprehend[26]. Let's maintain the good soil holding onto God to show us the next step to let the seed grow.

---

[25] Galatians 4:28-31
[26] Ephesians 3:20

Chapter 6

The Parable of the Lamp on the Stand

What is the Lamp on the Stand?

If the seed is the word of the Lord spoken to us and the soil is our ability to hear and grow God's word in our lives, let's look back again to Luke 8. Jesus follows the parable of the sower with the parable of the lamp on a stand. Again we often teach this as an exhortation to live our lives in such a way that people would see Jesus in us. This is a good interpretation of Matthew 5, but in light of Luke 8, I propose that it is also explaining the word of God.

"There is nothing hidden that will not be disclosed"[27]. Jesus is telling us that it is the nature of God to reveal things. He is the one putting things on the table. He is revealing things He wants us to know. Think of the time when the three strange visitors came to Abraham. This is commonly viewed as Jesus and maybe a couple of angels. After spending some time with Abraham, there are moving on to the city of Sodom. Abraham went with them seeing

---

[27] Luke 8:17

them on their way. Then the Lord said, "Shall I hide from Abraham what I am about to do"[28]?

God desires to communicate with us. Jesus tells us that He no longer calls us servants because a servant does not know his master's business. Instead, Jesus calls us friends because He tells us everything He learned from the Father[29].

Back in the parable of the lamp on a stand, Jesus highlights that this is about God's desire to speak by telling us to be careful how we listen[30]. God wants to share His secrets with us. The question is: will we listen and will it fall on good soil? If we do this, more will be given to us. God is looking for people wanting to hear Him speak.

Think about it. God has infinite wisdom and infinite knowledge. Can that well of having something to tell us ever dry up so we would not have to listen? He always has more to say. He always has more He wants to communicate.

When Isaiah had his heavenly experience, he heard the voice of the Lord "saying who will I send?"[31]. But, remember that when he first got

---

[28] Genesis 18:17
[29] John 15:15
[30] Luke 8:18
[31] Isaiah 6:1-6

there, Isaiah didn't hear those words; he was only aware of his sin. He was expecting to be killed or punished. God had to send an angel with a burning coal to touch his lips. This act allowed Isaiah to feel forgiven, and then without his focus on his guilt, Isaiah could hear what the voice of the Lord was speaking.

God didn't start speaking once Isaiah's sin was forgiven. It wasn't just a one-time word. God kept on saying it because He was waiting to find a person to respond to His request.

God is Always Speaking

God is always speaking, but at times we are too distracted with other things. Maybe we are like Isaiah and think God is too focused on our sin to speak about anything else. We may have feelings of unworthiness, thinking we are not anyone special that God would notice us. Our minds are filled with negative self-talk, and we think God is having those same thoughts about us. Nothing can be further from the truth - God loves us.

The enemy keeps telling us that we have run too far away from God's grace. He wants us to think there is more we need to do to earn God's love. Our enemy wants to fill our minds with these weeds, so that we will not hear the life-giving words from our loving Father.

When Jesus tells us in this parable to be careful how we listen, He wants us to know we have a choice whether we hear God or not. Will we focus on this negative self-talk fed to us by our enemy, or will we teach ourselves how to hear God's voice? If we wait to listen to God only when we need Him, we will not be prepared to hear His voice. Don't let your circumstances and experiences define God's plans for your life.

When your finances run low, what is God trying to say to you? When you get an unusual sickness, what does God want you to do? When people who said they would help you don't show up, what direction is God moving you? When your boss denies your promotion, does that end your time at that company? If God didn't withhold His very Son, but gave Him up for us, how will He not also graciously give us all things[32]? Let's expect God to want to speak His interpretation of the circumstances of our lives.

What are we going to believe to be true? Each of these things above has happened to us.

_____

[32] Romans 8:31-32

Our finances were low. I got a crazy dizziness that caused me to stay at home for several days. People who said they were coming to help our work changed their minds. And, for a season the Chinese government denied our request to stay in China.

Multiple times we had to go back to God to hear His word for us. His most common answer back to us was, "This can't not happen." When we were tempted to get discouraged, He would frequently remind us that He was in it. Our responsibility was to listen and believe.

When our world gets turned upside down, we need reminders that God is still in control. He wants to give us His perspective. Let's give Him opportunities to speak.

Who Are His Mother and Brothers?

The next story in Luke 8 is our transitional story and highlights the two main points of this book. Jesus' mother and brothers came to see Him but could not get through the crowds. When Jesus was informed of them being there, Jesus redefines who are truly His mother and brothers. He said, "My mother and brothers are those who hear God's word and put it into practice"[33].

Up to this point, we have looked specifically at God speaking and us preparing ourselves to listen. Now, Jesus adds a new point, once we have heard the voice of God, will we put it into practice?

Are you ready for the two ways to lead you to abundant living? They are not profound. In fact, they are quite easy to understand.

1. Listen to God.

2. Do what He says.

[33] Luke 8:21

Chapter 7

How to Live Abundantly

Jesus Calms the Sea

The rest of the chapter reveals what "putting it into practice" looks and how to do it. The first part of Luke 8 is teaching us to hear God's word; the latter part is how it looks to obey that word.

A quick view of the rest of the chapter seems to show how wonderful Jesus is and the great things He can do. I would suggest that while God is wonderful, the rest of this chapter is more profoundly teaching us how to live this same life.

In the first example after this transitional phrase about who His mother and brothers are, Jesus calms the storm. It must have been an amazing scene. The disciples are fearing death, and then Jesus does this thing that the disciples never dreamt could have been possible. "Who is this who even the wind and rain obey Him"[34]? Before they had time to take all this in, Jesus rebuked the disciples for their lack of faith.

---

[34] Mark 4:41

You have to ask why would this be Jesus' response. These were experienced fishermen. There was something about this storm that told them to be afraid. We are given every indication that if it wasn't for Jesus telling the storm to be quiet, they would have died. What then should they have done?

We know that Jesus only did what He saw His Father doing[35]. In the midst of the storm, He must have heard the Father speaking and seen the Father calming the sea. I believe His rebuke shows that the disciples could have heard the same word that Jesus did. They should have been looking for what the Father was doing. If they had seen it, and put it into practice, maybe they would have been the ones calming the sea.

Jesus Heals the Demoniac

Next we read the story of the man with a thousand demons. We see Jesus having a discussion with the demons, but we often miss verse 29. Jesus had commanded the impure spirits to come out, but they didn't.

If we believe that Jesus only did what He saw His Father doing, and only spoke what He

---

[35] John 5:19

heard His Father saying[36], we come to the conclusion that when He told those spirits to come out, He fully expected them to come out.

Many of us would have taken this response by the demons as evidence that it wasn't God's will. Many of us have no experience with talking to demons in this fashion, but we often give up on our prayers if the answer doesn't come soon. We may share our faith once, but give up because that person didn't give their life to Jesus. We allow the things we see to tell us what to believe.

Jesus was not dissuaded by those pressures of what He saw; He kept hold of the word of God had given and the seed which was planted that the man would be free. He knew the truth and kept pressing forward until He physically saw what He previously only knew by faith.

Jesus Gives Life to the Little Girl

I believe each of these examples in the second half of the chapter were revealing more to the disciples about hearing the word of God than just being amazed at all that Jesus could do. In the last example, Jesus raises a little girl

---

[36] John 5:19, 12:49

back to life. When He first reached the home of the synagogue leader, people were all saying that this girl was dead. Jesus was not influenced by the word they were saying and instead introduced a new word, "she is not dead but asleep"[37]. He heard the word of God, put it into practice by speaking it in faith, and then He commanded the girl to rise.

There are things we have all heard so much that we start to believe them. "China is a hard place." "It just the way things are." "I'll just have to deal with it." "I'm too old to learn Chinese." "There is so much we need to do."

Your words may be different. "I have wild kids." "I'm always making mistakes." "People can't be trusted." "I'll never get ahead." "Life sucks." You get the idea.

Let's stop voicing these words that lead to death and that take away our hope. Instead, let's go to God to get a new word from Him who makes all things possible. Let's not minimize what Jesus did on the cross - He changed everything. So when we hear a word or believe something that steals our hope and discourages us, it's not from God!

---

[37] Luke 8:52

If we are ever in a situation without hope, we don't have God's word for us in it. God's word comes to us to bring us life and life abundantly[38]. Even if the word is a to correct us, His word leads us to salvation and hope, not death[39]. Let's stop speaking out the words that steal our hope and focus on speaking those words from God that inspire us to believe all things are possible.

---

[38] John 10:10
[39] 2 Corinthians 7:11

Chapter 8

Now It's Our Turn

Now It's Our Turn

The last half of this chapter is awe-inspiring. We are left glorifying God and admiring Jesus. This is great since of course He is worthy of all praise and honor. However, I believe God designed this chapter to lead us to also listen for the word of God and, as Jesus showed us, put them into practice. It shows us how are we to walk out this same abundant life.

Do you doubt this? Does this seem too much of a stretch? Then take a look at how chapter 9 starts. Jesus sends out the twelve to do the same things they just saw Jesus doing[40].

Chapter 8 is preparing the disciples to do the work of ministry themselves. Jesus was telling them to listen to the voice of God and to step out in obedience. It's not doing whatever we think is best. It's not wishful thinking. There is a deliberate listening to what God is saying and watching for what He is doing. Then it is joining Him by speaking and doing those same

---

[40] Luke 9:1-9

things God is doing. There is demonstration of an outrageous faith that goes against what we may physically see to believe what we hear.

Jesus tells us who are His mother and brothers? Those who hear God's word and put it into practice. And, we are also His mothers and brothers. We are the family of God, the body of Christ, with Jesus as our head. God is continually calling us to listen to His word.

Therefore if we want this same power in our lives, then we must do what we can to prepare the good soil in our hearts to hold God's word to us. The first is making time to listen for the seed that God is speaking in our circumstances. The second is doing the hard work to maintain the good soil to allow the seed to grow. Will we believe the word of God and put that word into practice? The more we do this, the more God will speak to us[41]. That's the promise of God to us.

Where Are You in Terms of Hearing From God?

Maybe you need a new word from the Lord. Maybe you know the seed given to you, but you

---

[41] Luke 8:18

need to change from the soil mixed with thorns and thistles threatening to choke out God's seed. You need help pulling up the weeds and to speak life to God's word to find your hope. Maybe you know you have had soil as hard as the trampled path because God didn't come through before as you had hoped, and so you hardened your heart towards Him. Now you want recommit yourself to maintaining good soil, believing God is for you and wants what is good for you. Maybe you just need a touch from God.

If you get nothing else from this entire book, please know it is the heart of God to speak to you. He wants to be in relationship with you. He wants to comfort you and for you to know that He is for you. He says come to Me all who are weary and heavy-laden, and I will give you rest[42]. He will be with you always, even to the very end of the age[43]. Jesus promised us abundant life because He desires for us to have it. Let's open ourselves to hearing God's word to us and commit to putting it into practice.

---

[42] Matthew 11:28
[43] Matthew 28:20

About the Author

Kevin Shorter is a writer and teacher with the focus on leading himself and others into the heart of God the Father. You can join the more than 20,000 that follow him on either his blog, prayer-coach.com, Twitter @Prayer_Coach, or Facebook at PrayerCoachBlog.

Kevin and his wife, Allison, started the non-profit, Josiah's Covenant, which aimed to create families for Asian orphans, provide them with job opportunities, teach them life skills, and keep them from being caught in the sex trade. This ministry has now been handed off to locals who are actively running it.

Other Books by the Author

Academy of Powerful Caregivers: Staying Motivated in Ministry

Breaking Free: How to Be Completely Free From Any Addiction

3,500+ Prayer Quotes: Inspiration to Draw You Closer to God

Creative Intercession: How Simplicity, Fun, and Art Can Move the Hand of God

Church Search: How to Get Your Ministry to Show Up in Search Engines

One Last Thing...

If you enjoyed this book, please consider writing a review or sharing it with your friends. This would be greatly appreciated. Thanks.

www.ingramcontent.com/pod-product-compliance
Lightning Source LLC
Chambersburg PA
CBHW020608030426
42337CB00013B/1274